NEW YORK

In the 1650s, about 500 people lived in the quiet little Dutch town of New Amsterdam. Now, in the twenty-first century, New Amsterdam is the city of New York. Seven and a half million people live there, and more than twenty million people come to visit it every year.

Why do they come? They want to see the New York of Jennifer Lopez, George Gershwin, and King Kong. They want to visit some of New York's fine museums, or shop in Macy's and Bloomingdales. They want to eat hot dogs, take the Staten Island ferry, see the Statue of Liberty, and remember 9/11.

There are hundreds of things to do in New York. What do *you* want to do? Your tour begins here . . .

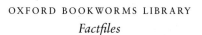

OXFORD BOOKWORMS LIBRARY
Factfiles

New York

Stage 1 (400 headwords)

Factfiles Series Editor: Christine Lindop

JOHN ESCOTT

New York

OXFORD UNIVERSITY PRESS

OXFORD
UNIVERSITY PRESS

Great Clarendon Street, Oxford OX2 6DP

Oxford University Press is a department of the University of Oxford.
It furthers the University's objective of excellence in research, scholarship,
and education by publishing worldwide in

Oxford New York

Auckland Cape Town Dar es Salaam Hong Kong Karachi
Kuala Lumpur Madrid Melbourne Mexico City Nairobi
New Delhi Shanghai Taipei Toronto

With offices in

Argentina Austria Brazil Chile Czech Republic France Greece
Guatemala Hungary Italy Japan Poland Portugal Singapore
South Korea Switzerland Thailand Turkey Ukraine Vietnam

OXFORD and OXFORD ENGLISH are registered trade marks of
Oxford University Press in the UK and in certain other countries

ISBN: 978 0 19 423373 6

A complete recording of this Bookworms edition of
New York is available.

Printed in China

Word count (main text): 4,640

For more information on the Oxford Bookworms Library,
visit www.oup.com/elt/gradedreaders

The publishers would like to thank the following for permission to reproduce images:

Alamy pp viii (The Hoberman Collection), 21 (Christopher Hill), 22-23 (Frances M Roberts), 24
(Black Star/Flea Market, Gavin Gough/Hot dog stand); Bridgeman Art Library p 2 (Collection of the
New York Historical Society); Corbis pp 10 (RF/Statue of Liberty), 30 (Seth Wenig), 36 (Shannon
Stapleton); Empics pp 9 (AP/Dima Gavrysh), 34 (Mary Altaffer); Gamma pp 27 (David Lefranc), 28-29
(David Lefranc/Times Square); Getty Images pp 5 (Hirz), 8, 11 (George Eastman House/Lewis W.
Hine), 20 (Liason Agency/Chris Hondros), 25 (Brad Barket), 26 (Paul Hawthorne), 28 (Bryan Bedder/
Comedy Club), 31 (Nick Laham), 32, 33 (Chris Trotman), 38 (Ted Russell); The Kobal Collection
p 1 (Marvel/Sony Pictures); Magnum Photos pp 7 (Steve McCurry) 12-13 (Stuart Franklin), 49 (Erich
Hartmann); Museum of New York City p 4; Pictures Colour Library pp 16, 17; Reuters p 40 (Peter
Morgan); Rex Features pp 15, 19 (Action Press), 37 (Sipa Press); Robert Harding Picture Library
pp 10 (Neil Emmerson/ cabs), 18 (C. Rennie), 35 (Sylvain Grandadam); Topfoto pp 14 (The Image
Works/Michael J.Doolittle), 39 (The Image Works/Monika Graff)

This book is printed on paper from certified and well-managed sources.

CONTENTS

1 The Big Apple

More than twenty million people from all over the world visit New York every year. Most of them say, 'It's the most exciting city in the world!' They know many of the streets, avenues, and famous buildings before they come. How do they know them? From American movies, old and new – *King Kong, On the Town, Annie, Manhattan, Spiderman,* and many more.

New York is not the capital of New York State. Albany, 154 miles to the north of the city, is the capital. But New York is much more famous than Albany. People often call it 'The Big Apple'. Why? In the 1920s and 1930s, jazz musicians in the United States all wanted to work in New York.

Spiderman in New York

'There are a lot of apples on the tree,' they said, 'but when you take New York City, you take The Big Apple!'

Lots of famous people live or lived in New York: actors the Marx Brothers, Robert De Niro, Al Pacino, Whoopi Goldberg, and Tom Cruise; musicians Christina Aguilera, Alicia Keys, 50 Cent, Jennifer Lopez, Jerome Kern, and George Gershwin.

Yes, everybody wanted some of The Big Apple – and they want some today, too!

When visitors think about New York, they usually think about Manhattan – an island 13 ½ miles long and 2 miles across. But New York has five boroughs: Manhattan, Brooklyn, the Bronx, Queens, and Staten Island. The city has 6,500 miles of streets, and seven and a half million people live there. Another three and a half million people travel in to New York to work every day.

But New York was not always a big city . . .

2   In the beginning

Four hundred years ago, Manhattan Island was the home of the Native American people called the Algonquin Indians. In 1609, a man called Henry Hudson came up the river to Manhattan. He was British but he was on a Dutch ship, the *Half Moon*. Today, that river is called the Hudson River.

In 1626, a Dutchman called Peter Minuit gave the Algonquin Indians about twenty-four dollars for the island of Manhattan. Minuit built some houses, and called the little town New Amsterdam after the city of Amsterdam in the Netherlands. Twenty years later, about 500 people lived there.

The Algonquin Indians and Peter Minuit

But in 1664, the British took the town from the Dutch and changed its name to New York. Then there was the War of Independence (1775–1783) – a war between the British and some of the people of North America. It finished in 1783, the British left, and the United States of America had its first president – George Washington.

In 1790, about 33,000 people lived in New York, but then millions more men and women began to leave their countries and come to America from all over the world. These immigrants all wanted to be part of the new country, and many of them wanted to live in New York. The first immigrants came from Germany and Ireland; later, more came from Italy, Poland, Czechoslovakia, Russia, Africa, and China.

These 'New Americans' often lived in the same streets with other people from their own country – Irish with

Building Brooklyn Bridge

Building a skyscraper

Irish, Italians with Italians, Chinese with Chinese. Today, there are parts of New York called Chinatown and Little Italy.

The immigrants worked very hard, and many of them helped to build the first skyscrapers and bridges. Brooklyn Bridge, more than 6,000 feet long, opened on 24 May 1883. Thousands of New Yorkers watched, and 150,300 people went across the bridge on the first day.

In 1898, the five boroughs made a new city. Manhattan, Brooklyn, Queens, the Bronx and Staten Island were now New York City – the second largest city in the world.

The 1920s are often called the 'roaring twenties'. With dancing, jazz, the first talking movies – America was an exciting place. And nowhere was more exciting than New York. From 1920 to 1933 people could not make or sell alcohol in New York – but of course you *could* find it in dark streets or behind the doors of small clubs.

In 1930 the Chrysler Building opened, then the Empire State Building in 1931. For many years, it was the tallest building in the city – until 1972, when the World Trade Center was built.

The two skyscrapers of the World Trade Center, on Church Street and Liberty Street, were the tallest buildings in New York. There were more than one hundred floors, with offices, shops, and restaurants inside. The 'Windows on the World' restaurant was one of the most famous restaurants in the city.

But on 11 September, 2001 – '9/11' to Americans – everything changed. At 8.46 a.m. on that day an American Airlines plane crashed into the North Tower of the World Trade Center. Seventeen minutes later, at 9.03 a.m., a United Airlines plane crashed into the South Tower.

Nobody can forget 9/11. People all across the world watched on TV and saw the last minutes of the two big towers. Thousands of people died in and near the Center.

Today this place is called Ground Zero. Many visitors to New York like to go there and remember 9/11. It is one more story – one of the unhappiest stories – from this city.

The World Trade Center, 9/11

3   Visiting the city

Travel is easy in Manhattan. There are twelve avenues, First to Twelfth, and they go north and south. Sixth Avenue also has a name – the Avenue of the Americas. Most streets go east and west, and after 14th Street the streets and avenues go in straight lines. The East Side is to the east of Fifth Avenue, and the West Side is to the west of it.

Lots of New Yorkers travel under the streets and buildings of New York on subway trains. When you take the subway, ask yourself, 'Where am I going – uptown (north) or downtown (south)?' You can buy a MetroCard

The straight avenues of New York

The subway

at subway stations or at more than 3,000 other places around the city. Visitors can also buy a one-day Fun Pass and travel with it all day.

The subway is noisy and dirty, but it's cheap and quick. Millions of people take the subway trains to and from work every day. Some trains go for twenty-four hours a day.

When you want to go by bus, you can buy a MetroCard. Or you can get on the bus first and put the right money in the box next to the driver. There are buses on most avenues and on the bigger streets. There are buses twenty-four hours each day, but sometimes you can wait a long time for a bus between midnight and 6 a.m.

Yellow cabs

There are more than 12,000 yellow taxis – called yellow cabs – in New York. You can usually find a cab near the big hotels, and you can stop them in the street.

There is a ferry from Battery Park to the Statue of Liberty and Ellis Island. The Staten Island ferry also leaves from Battery Park. It leaves every twenty to thirty minutes, twenty-four hours a day. And it's free for everybody!

For some of the best views of the city, take a Circle Line boat around the island of Manhattan. You can learn a lot about the city, and you can see views of the other four boroughs of New York.

Or go in a helicopter and look *down* on the skyscrapers! Helicopters leave from West 30th Street and Twelfth Avenue, and from Pier 6, the East River.

The people of France gave the Statue of Liberty to the American people in 1886. The statue is about 150 feet high, and her arm is 42 feet long. From the tenth floor there are wonderful views of New York. Get your ticket from the ticket office at

The Statue of Liberty

Immigrants arriving at Ellis Island

Battery Park before you get on the ferry. There is also a museum on Liberty Island.

Between 1892 and 1954, Ellis Island was the first stop for nearly 17 million immigrants. All the ships from Europe stopped here. Many famous people came through Ellis Island – Isaac Asimov, Samuel Goldwyn, Rudolf Valentino, Sigmund Freud, Charlie Chaplin and Walt Disney. Today, you can take a ferry boat across the river and visit Ellis Island. Here, in the museum, you can see pictures of many of those immigrants.

South Street Seaport is by the East River. It tells the story of New York, the sea, and the rivers. It is full of shops, restaurants, museums, and ships old and new.

4   Around Manhattan

South of Canal Street and west of Chatham Square is New York's Chinatown. Chinese people first came to New York around 1850. Most of them were men; they lived and worked in New York, and sent money home to their families. Many helped to build the railways in California and across the West before they came to New York.

Today, more than 80,000 Chinese-Americans live in Chinatown. There are many interesting shops here, and when you want to eat or drink, there are restaurants and tea-shops everywhere – nearly 400 of them.

Little Italy is north of Canal Street and west of the Bowery. It was once the home of thousands of Italian immigrants, and now it has some of the best Italian restaurants in the city.

Each year in September there is the Festival of San Gennaro. Three million people come every year to enjoy the eleven days of the festival.

The Festival of San Gennaro, Little Italy

There is a lot of music, and very good Italian food too. A big parade goes along Mulberry and Mott Streets, between Canal and Houston Streets, on 19 September.

Greenwich Village is west of Broadway, between 14th Street and Houston Street. It got its name from Greenwich in south-east London when the British were in New York before the War of Independence. Many famous artists and writers lived in the old houses on the little streets of Greenwich Village; Edgar Allan Poe, Mark Twain, Jackson Pollock, Jack Kerouac, and Allen Ginsberg all lived here. There are interesting shops, cafés, art galleries, jazz clubs, and theatres.

At 75½ Bedford Street you can see New York's smallest house. It is just 9½ feet across, and it was built in 1873.

Jefferson Market Courthouse, at 425 Sixth Avenue, is one of America's ten most beautiful buildings. It has a beautiful tower with big clocks.

Central Park is between Fifth Avenue and Central Park West, and from 59th to 110th Streets. It is six per cent of Manhattan! In this quiet place you can get away from the people and the noise of the city. It has a big lake, hundreds of trees, and beautiful gardens. Often there is music in the park too. Visit the Delacorte Theatre or the Central Park Zoo, or take a tour of Central Park by bicycle. New Yorkers love to walk, run, skate and play in Central Park; it gets the most visitors of any park in the United States.

Central Park

5   Great buildings

The Empire State Building at Fifth Avenue and 34th Street is New York's tallest skyscraper. Between 1931 and 1972, it was the tallest building in the world.

Work on the building started in 1930, and it opened in 1931. It is 1,250 feet high and has 102 floors. In 1933 people all over the world saw the Empire State Building in the movie *King Kong*.

The Empire State Building

You can go up to the 86th floor for wonderful views of the city. In 1945 a plane flew over Manhattan and hit the 79th floor of the building. Fourteen people died in the accident.

The United Nations Building is by the East River at First Avenue and 45th Street. It has beautiful gardens by the river. People from more than 190 countries meet and work here. There are tours most days, and you can see some interesting statues in the gardens.

Every day, trains take half a million people to and from the Grand Central Terminal on East 42nd Street at Park Avenue. This wonderful building opened in 1913. The main part is 275 feet long and 125 feet high. Look up at the beautiful blue ceiling with its 2,500 stars. The windows are 60 feet high. The Grand Central Oyster Bar is one of New York's most famous restaurants, and there are lots more restaurants, cafés and shops. There are free tours on Wednesdays and Fridays.

The Rockefeller Center is between Fifth and Seventh Avenues and 47th and 51st Streets. New Yorkers love to come here at Christmas. Here there are shops, restaurants, and cafés. There is also the famous Radio City Music Hall – the largest theatre in the world. The Center was built between 1931 and 1940. In the winter, you can skate on the Lower Plaza. And at Christmas there is always a big Christmas tree at the Rockefeller Center. It is usually between 75 and 90 feet high.

Skating at the Rockefeller Center

6 Museums and galleries

There are more than sixty museums in Manhattan. Some stay open late one or two evenings in the week, and some are free.

The Metropolitan Museum of Art – '5,000 years of art' – is New York's biggest museum, and is on Fifth Avenue. It has three floors with thousands of paintings, statues and other things. Titian, El Greco, Monet, Cezanne, and Rousseau are just some of the names in the Metropolitan Museum. There is a garden of statues too.

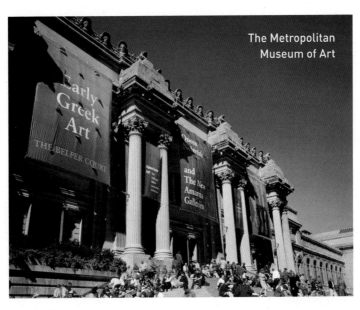

The Metropolitan Museum of Art

Perhaps you are interested in American artists. At the Whitney Museum of American Art at 945 Madison Avenue you can see pictures by Edward Hopper, Georgia O'Keeffe, Jasper Johns, William de Kooning and many more American artists.

The Museum of Modern Art (MOMA) is at 11 West 53rd Street. It has the world's biggest collection of modern art. There are six floors of pictures, photographs, and statues. Two of the most famous pictures are Monet's *Water Lilies* and Picasso's *Les Demoiselles d'Avignon*.

The Museum of the City of New York on Fifth Avenue, at 103rd Street, tells the story of New York from its beginning. Watch the *Timescapes* movie, and visit the exhibition *Perform* about New York theatre.

The Guggenheim Museum is also on Fifth Avenue, at 88th Street. This museum opened in 1959. You can see

The Guggenheim Museum

the work of Picasso, Kandinsky, Modigliani, and other modern artists in this strange but wonderful building.

The American Museum of the Moving Image is on Thirty-Fifth Avenue at 36th Street, Astoria, Queens. From Manhattan it is about a fifteen-minute ride on the subway. You can see more than 85,000 different things from the movies – clothes from *Chicago* and *Star Trek*, photos of movie stars, and much more. You can learn about movies and television, and watch movies in the museum's theatre.

Would you like to see something different? At the New York City Police Museum at 100 Old Slip between South

The New York City Police Museum

and Water Streets you can learn all about New York's police – their work, their cars, and their clothes (from 1626 to today). At the Intrepid Sea-Air-Space Museum – Pier 86, Hudson River at 46th Street – you can visit US ships, planes, and helicopters. At the Museum of Television and Radio at 25 West 52nd Street, between Fifth and Sixth Avenues, you can listen to radio programmes and watch TV programmes – 120,000 of them! You can also watch movies in the museum's theatre. And the International Center of Photography at 1133 Sixth Avenue at 43rd Street has thousands of photos from the earliest times up to today, and exhibitions of old and new work.

7 Shopping and eating

People love to go shopping in New York. You can find nearly everything here, and sometimes things are very cheap. And there are shopping tours! Most of New York's biggest shops are in midtown Manhattan. Fifth Avenue has some of the biggest names – Tiffany's, Cartier, Saks Fifth Avenue, Bergdorf Goodman, Lord and Taylor, Gucci, Lacoste. Or go to the wonderful Trump Tower with its shops and restaurants.

Macy's – 'The World's Largest Store' – is on Broadway and 34th Street. For men's clothes, go to Brooks Brothers

or Paul Stuart, on Madison Avenue. For women's clothes, try Betsey Johnson at 248 Columbus Avenue or Calvin Klein at 654 Madison Avenue.

There are more clothes at American Apparel at 183 Houston Street, Urban Outfitters at 628 Broadway between Bleeker and Houston Streets, Mr Joe at 500 Eighth Avenue between 35th and 36th Streets and Levi's (famous for their jeans) at 536 Broadway between Prince and Spring Streets.

For cheap clothes, go to Century 21 at 22 Cortlandt Street between Broadway and Church Street. And Hell's Kitchen Flea Market, at West 39th Street between Ninth and Tenth Avenues, and Avenue A Flea Market at 11th Street are both open on Saturdays and Sundays.

For CDs and other music, go to Tower Records at

Shops on Fifth Avenue

1961 Broadway or Midnight Records 263 West 23rd Street. Are you looking for something old or different? Then visit Gryphon Records at 233 West 72nd Street, House of Oldies at 35 Carmine Street, or Other Music at 15 East 4th Street.

And there are bookshops. Barnes and Noble on Fifth Avenue has more than three million books. The Strand Book

A flea market

Store at 828 Broadway sells new and old books. Readers of mystery books can find thousands and thousands of them at Murder Ink at 2486 Broadway and the Mysterious Bookshop at 129 West 56th Street. Gotham Book Mart at 41 West 47th Street has hundreds of old books.

A food stand

For 'something different', go to SoHo (between Canal Street and West Houston Street) or Greenwich Village. For everything Chinese, go to Pearl River Mart at 477 Broadway between Broome and Grand Streets.

You never need to be hungry in New York! There are more than 25,000 restaurants, cafés, 'fast food' shops, and food stands in New York's five boroughs. You can find something for everyone – from the cheapest to the most expensive – and you can eat food from every country in the world. But remember – when you buy food in America, in a restaurant or on the street, you usually get a lot!

New Yorkers often eat at the delicatessen – or 'deli'. These food shops sell wonderful sandwiches. There are fast food stands on many streets. These sell food like hamburgers and hot dogs, and drinks like Coca-Cola.

From 3 p.m. to 5 p.m. you can have 'afternoon tea' at one of the bigger hotels – the Plaza at 768 Fifth Avenue, the Waldorf-Astoria at 301 Park Avenue or the Carlyle at 35 East 76th Street.

A New York 'deli'

8 Nights out in the city

Some of the best actors, singers, and dancers in the world live and work in New York. Most of the theatres are in the streets near Times Square and on Broadway, between 41st and 53rd Streets. There are thirty or more theatres on Broadway, and tickets are expensive, but sometimes you can get cheaper tickets on the day.

'Off-Broadway' theatres are cheaper, and you can get a ticket more easily. You can find off-Broadway theatres in Greenwich Village and in some other parts of New York.

And sometimes you can watch things for free! Bryant Park Free Summer Season in Bryant Park, Sixth Avenue at

A concert in Central Park

42nd Street is between June and August. In the evenings you can watch movies, at lunchtimes watch theatre, and at weekends listen to concerts. And you can hear free concerts at Central Park SummerStage at Rumsey Playfield in Central Park, between June and September.

The Lincoln Center is on Broadway and 64th Street. Here you can see dancing or listen to music. You can also listen to music at Carnegie Hall on 57th Street and Seventh Avenue, and at Radio City Music Hall at 1260 Sixth Avenue.

New York is a wonderful city for jazz. You can hear some of the best jazz at the Blue Note at 131 West 3rd Street, Village Vanguard at 178 Seventh Avenue South, and at Birdland at 315 West 44th Street.

For rock music, try the Mercury Lounge at 217 East Houston Street, Irving Plaza at 17 Irving Place at 15th Street, S.O.B's at 204 Varick Street, the Hammerstein Ballroom at 311 West 34th Street, The Living Room at 154 Ludlow Street or Maxwell's at 1039 Washington Street. Sometimes you can hear a rock concert at Madison Square Garden at Eighth Avenue and 33rd Street.

A comedy club

There are lots of Irish people in New York, and they love music. You can hear Irish music at Blaggards Pub, 8 West 38th Street, or at Connolly's in Times Square.

There are cinemas – often called movie theatres – all over the city, and people make a lot of movies on the streets of New York too. Woody Allen is probably New York's most famous movie-maker. The New York Film Festival begins at the end of September for two weeks at the Lincoln Center. You can see new movies from America and other countries for the first time.

Nightclubs are good places for an evening out, but they can be expensive. Go to the Rainbow

Room at 30 Rockefeller Plaza. Or there is the Supper Club at 240 West 47th Street.

For lots of laughs, go to the Comedy Cellar at 117 MacDougal Street between Bleeker and West 3rd Streets or to Carolines on Broadway at 1626 Broadway between 49th and 50th Streets.

Bars and clubs, midnight movies, late-night shops, and food stands in the street. 'This city never sleeps,' New Yorkers say.

Late-night New York

9 Outside Manhattan

New York is more than just Manhattan. There are four more boroughs in the city– Brooklyn, Queens, the Bronx, and Staten Island.

Brooklyn is one of the oldest parts of New York, and it has many interesting old buildings. Many visitors (and many New Yorkers too) like to visit Coney Island. In this part of South Brooklyn there are more than three miles of beaches. And you can have an exciting time at the amusement park. For children, there is the Brooklyn

Coney Island Amusement Park

Tennis at Flushing Meadows

Children's Museum, at 145 Brooklyn Avenue. It was the first children's museum in the world.

Flushing Meadows-Corona Park is in Queens. The 50,000-seat Shea Stadium, home of the New York Mets baseball team, is here. Flushing Meadows is the home of the US National Tennis Center.

Queens has many museums and restaurants. Take the Number 7 subway from Times Square to Flushing. The train takes you above the roads and houses and gives you one of the best views of New York.

Two interesting places in the Bronx are the Bronx Zoo and the New York Botanical Garden. The zoo opened in

1899. Today it has more than seven thousand animals. It also has a children's zoo and a big park. The New York Botanical Garden has forty-eight gardens, and a garden for children.

Take the free ferry to Staten Island, south of Manhattan. Staten Island has some beautiful old New York buildings, and there are lakes and hills with good views of New York and the rivers. Historic Richmond Town is at 441 Clarke Avenue. In this museum village you can visit twenty-seven different buildings. One is from the 1690s, and another from the 1820s. Also on Staten Island is the Chinese Scholar's Garden – a quiet, beautiful, green place in a noisy city.

The New York Botanical Garden

10 From baseball to tennis

Americans love to watch baseball, and New York has two famous baseball teams – the Mets and the Yankees. Shea Stadium is the home of the New York Mets, and they play there between April and September.

The New York Knicks basketball team play at Madison Square Garden from October to April.

Madison Square Garden is also the place for ice hockey, between October and April. The city's oldest team, the New York Rangers, play here.

Baseball

The city's two football teams – American football, of course – are the New York Giants and the New York Jets. See them at the Giants Stadium in New Jersey.

In November every year, 25,000 people run through all five boroughs of New York in the New York Marathon. They begin on Staten Island, and finish 26 miles and 385 yards later in Central Park.

You can ride a horse at the Claremont Riding Academy at 175 West 89th Street, or in Central Park. You can get

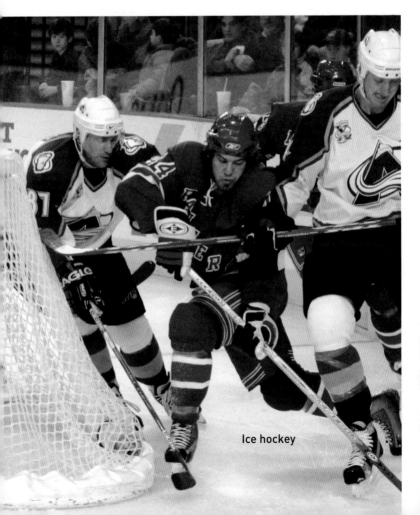

Ice hockey

bikes for about ten dollars an hour in the park too. There are no cars in the park on Saturdays and Sundays, so people like riding and walking then.

Runners can go to the Central Park Reservoir running track, or to Chelsea Piers Sports and Entertainment Complex, Piers 59–62 at 23rd Street and Eleventh Avenue.

Tennis players from all over the world come to the National Tennis Center at Flushing Meadows, Queens, for the US Open Tennis Championships. These are in early September.

The New York Marathon

11   We love a parade!

New Yorkers love parades and there is one in some part of the city most months of the year. One of the biggest is the St Patrick's Day Parade.

St Patrick's Day Parade is on 17 March. It is the longest, oldest, and most famous of all the New York parades. It started in 1762. It goes along Fifth Avenue from 44th Street to 86th Street. More than 150,000 people walk in the parade.

In March or April the Ringling Brothers and Barnum and Bailey Circus comes to the city. On the first and last nights of the circus, there is a parade with the circus animals from the Queens Midtown Tunnel to

St Patrick's Day Parade

Madison Square Garden at midnight.

Circus clowns

There is an Easter Parade on Fifth Avenue on Easter Sunday, from 49th to 57th Streets.

America's Independence Day is on 4 July. There are many street parades and fireworks in the five boroughs of New York.

On 31 October is the Halloween Parade. This began as a walk for children on Halloween night in Greenwich Village. It is now a big parade for everyone.

The first Macy's Thanksgiving Day Parade was in 1924. It is on the last Thursday in November and goes along Broadway from 77th Street to 34th Street. The parade can be 2½ miles long. Some people get up very early and wait for hours for the parade.

At Christmas you can go to Radio City Music Hall for their wonderful Christmas Show, or go skating at the Rockefeller Center.

Late on New Year's Eve (31 December), many people go to Times Square. At midnight, everyone sings and dances and says 'Happy New Year!' to their friends or the people near them. There are fireworks in Central Park and a midnight run through the park.

Perhaps you're thinking about a visit to New York. What other things do visitors need to know? People often ask, 'Is New York dangerous?' No more dangerous

Fireworks on Independence Day

than any other big city. There are a lot of police on the streets of New York too. Just be careful – don't carry a lot of money with you, and stay with other people late at night.

Some visitors find that New Yorkers are not very friendly. Some are, some aren't. Some taxi drivers talk a lot, but others only say 'Yeah!' or 'OK!' when you talk to them.

New York can be very hot in the middle of summer and very cold in the middle of winter. Take the right clothes with you when you visit.

The city is always changing. You can hear the noise of building work all the time. Cars and buses stop and start,

Times Square on New Year's Eve

and yellow cabs are everywhere. WALK and DON'T WALK signs go on and off, and people run between streets and avenues.

That's New York.

That's the most exciting city in the world.

GLOSSARY

alcohol strong drinks like wine, beer or whisky

art pictures and other beautiful things that people like to look at

artist someone who paints or draws pictures

basketball a game for two teams of five players who try to throw a ball into a high net

boat a small ship for travelling on water

borough one part of a city

bus a kind of big 'car' which many people can travel in

buy to give money for something

capital (city) the most important city in a country

circus a show with people and animals that goes from place to place

clothes things you wear, e.g. shirts, trousers, dresses

club a place where you go to dance and listen to music

collection a group of things of the same kind in one place

crash to hit something hard and noisily

dance to move your body to music

dangerous something dangerous can hurt or kill you

exhibition a number of things people go to look at e.g. in a museum or gallery

ferry a boat that takes people or things on short journeys across a river

floor one level of a building

food what you eat

gallery a place where you can see paintings and other kinds of art

helicopter a kind of small plane that can go straight up into the air

immigrant a person who comes to another country to live there

island a piece of land with water around it

lake an area of water with land around it

modern of the present time

museum a place where you can look at old or interesting things

music   when you sing or play an instrument, you make music

musician   a person who makes music

mystery   a kind of book about crimes and strange events

park   a large place with trees and gardens where people can go to walk, play games etc.

part   one of the pieces of something

railway   the metal lines that trains go on from one place to another

restaurant   a place where people can buy and eat meals

ride   to sit on a horse and make it move; to travel in a car or train

saint (St)   part of the name of a very good or holy person; often written as St

sell   to give something to someone and get money for it

team   a group of people who play a sport together against another group

theatre   a building where you go to see plays

tour   a short visit to see a building or city

travel   to go from one place to another place

view   what you can see from a certain place

war   fighting between countries or groups of people

zoo   a place where you can see wild animals in a town or city

New York

ACTIVITIES

ACTIVITIES

Before Reading

1 Read the back cover of the book, and the introduction on the first page. How much do you know now about New York? Are these sentences true (T) or false (F)?

1 Twenty-five million people live in New York.

2 More than twenty million people visit New York every year.

3 In the 1650s New York was called Little London.

4 You can visit the Statue of Lord Nelson.

5 You can see a show in a Broadway theatre.

6 New York is small, quiet, and boring.

2 Which of these places are you going to find in a book about New York? Tick six of the twelve boxes.

☐ Niagara Falls   ☐ Macy's
☐ Harrods   ☐ The White House
☐ Central Park   ☐ Brooklyn
☐ Big Ben   ☐ Manhattan
☐ The Eiffel Tower   ☐ The Colosseum
☐ The Staten Island Ferry   ☐ Coney Island

Which other places do you know in New York?

Which places in New York would you most like to visit?

ACTIVITIES

While Reading

Read Chapters 1 and 2. Are these sentences true (T) or false (F)? Change the false sentences into true ones.

1 Manhattan is an island, thirteen and a half miles long.
2 New York has five boroughs.
3 The city has 7,500 miles of streets.
4 George Hudson was the first president of the United States of America.
5 The first immigrants came from Germany and Ireland.
6 There is a part of New York called Little China.
7 From 1920 to 1933 people could not make or sell alcohol in New York.
8 For many years, the Chrysler Building was the tallest in the city.

Read Chapter 3, and then complete these sentences with the right words.

avenues, cabs, ferry, immigrants, people, subway, views

1 There are twelve _____ in New York.
2 The _____ is noisy, dirty, cheap, and quick.
3 Taxis are called yellow _____ in New York.
4 There are wonderful _____ of New York from the Statue of Liberty.
5 The _____ of France gave the statue to the Americans in 1886.
6 You can take a _____ and visit Ellis Island.
7 Ellis Island was the first stop for all the _____ from Europe.

Read Chapters 4 and 5, then answer these questions.

1 When did Chinese people first come to New York?
2 Where are the best Italian restaurants in the city?
3 When is the Festival of San Gennaro?
4 What can you see at 75½ Bedford Street?
5 Where can you find a lake in New York?
6 When did the Empire State Building open?
7 Where do people from more than 190 countries meet and work?
8 Where are the windows 60 feet high?
9 Which is the largest theatre in the world?
10 Where is there a big tree at Christmas?

Read Chapter 6, then match the beginnings and the endings of the sentences.

1 The Metropolitan Museum of Art is . . .
2 The Museum of Modern Art has . . .
3 At the Museum of the City of New York watch . . .
4 The Guggenheim Museum opened . . .
5 The American Museum of the Moving Image has . . .
6 At the Intrepid Sea-Air-Space Museum you can see . . .
7 At the Museum of Television and Radio you can watch . . .

a the *Timescapes* movie.
b New York's biggest museum.
c US ships, planes, and helicopters.
d 120,000 TV programmes.
e in 1959.
f the world's biggest collection of modern art.
g 85,000 different things from movies.

Read Chapter 7. Match the places with the things you can eat or buy there.

1	Brooks Brothers	a	afternoon tea
2	Betsey Johnson	b	women's clothes
3	Hell's Kitchen Flea Market	c	everything Chinese
4	Barnes and Noble	d	men's clothes
5	Pearl River Mart	e	cheap clothes
6	Waldorf Astoria	f	books

Read Chapter 8. Match the places with the things you can see or hear there.

1	Broadway	a	movies
2	Central Park SummerStage	b	rock music
3	Blue Note	c	jazz
4	Mercury Lounge	d	theatre
5	Connolly's	e	free concerts
6	New York Film Festival	f	Irish music

Read Chapters 9, 10, and 11. Complete the sentences with the names of the places.

1 At _____ Island there are more than three miles of beach.

2 The _____ Zoo opened in 1899.

3 _____ Stadium is the home of the New York Mets.

4 The New York Marathon begins on _____ Island.

5 There are no cars in _____ Park on Saturdays and Sundays.

6 The St Patrick's Day Parade goes along _____ Avenue.

7 Go to _____ Music Hall for their wonderful Christmas Show.

8 On New Year's Eve, many people go to _____ Square.

ACTIVITIES

After Reading

1 Martin is visiting New York. Read his e-mail and circle the correct words.

From: Martin
Subject: New York

Hello / Goodbye from New York

I *arrived / left* here on Friday. I caught the *train / plane* to *Grand Central Terminal / Victoria Station* and then the *tube / subway* to my hotel. It is next to *Hyde Park / Central Park* in the centre of the city. The *views / sights* from my window are wonderful.

Yesterday I went for a *walk / ride* on the Staten Island *ferry / train* to see the *Statue of Liberty / Eiffel Tower*. The people of *Britain / France* gave it to the Americans. It is very big! For lunch we had a *sandwich / afternoon tea* in a famous New York deli.

Last night I went to a famous theatre on *Broadway / Sixth Avenue*, and I saw a very exciting play. After the play I took a *yellow / red* cab back to my hotel.

Tomorrow I am going to *see / watch* the *movies / paintings* at the *Louvre / Metropolitan Museum of Art*. Then I am going shopping in *Harrods / Macy's*.

On Monday I am coming home.

See you soon.
Martin

2 Here is a new photo for the book. Find the best place in the book to put the picture, and answer these questions.

The picture goes on page _____.

1 Where was the photographer?
2 What are the people doing?
3 Who are the people in the pictures on the walls?
4 Would you like to visit this place?

Now write a caption for the photo.

Caption: _____

3 Use the clues below to complete this crossword with words from the story. Then find the hidden ten-letter word in the crossword.

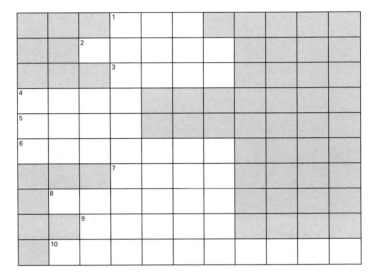

1 To give money for something.
2 To move your body to music.
3 To give something to someone and get money for it.
4 A large place with trees and gardens where people can go and walk, play games etc.
5 To sit on a horse and make it move; to travel in a car or train.
6 Things that you wear, e.g. shirts, trousers, dresses.
7 A small ship for travelling on water.
8 To go from one place to another place.
9 One level of a building.
10 A kind of small plane that can go straight up into the air.

The hidden word in the crossword is _____.

4　Here is a paragraph about New York. Write the correct words in the spaces.

Central Park, Ellis Island, Empire State Building, ferry, Fifth Avenue, hot dogs, north-east, paintings, seven, subway, theatres, twenty

New York is in the _____ of the United States of America. More than _____ million people live there and _____ million people visit the city every year. They like to travel on the _____, see the _____ in the museums and see the wonderful views from the _____. They also like to eat _____ and walk in _____. Many people take the _____ to _____ . They also want to go shopping on _____ . In the evening the _____ on Broadway are very popular.

Now write a paragraph about a city in your country. Begin . . .

(My city) _____ is in the _____ of _____. It has _____ million people.

Now compare New York and your city. Which things are the same? Which things are different? What is the most interesting thing about each city? Where would you like to live? Why?

5　Imagine you are going to visit New York for a weekend. What five things would you most like to see and do there? What would you like to visit first? What would you like to buy, and which food would you like to try? What is the most interesting thing about the city for you? You can find more information about the city at www.nycvisit.com.

ABOUT THE AUTHOR

John Escott worked in business before becoming a writer. Since then he has written many books for readers of all ages. He was born in Somerset, in the west of England, but now lives in Bournemouth in the south. From here he can easily reach the Dorset coast, which, he says, is his favourite part of England. When he is not working, he likes looking for long-forgotten books in small backstreet bookshops, watching old Hollywood films, and walking for miles along empty beaches.

He has visited New York several times. Two of his favourite places are the Guggenheim Museum and the Trump Tower. He also enjoyed the Circle Line boat tour, and the trip to Ellis Island, where he liked reading the sad stories from the lives of early immigrants to the United States.

He has written or retold more than twenty stories for Oxford Bookworms, from Starter to Stage 6, and he has also written for the Oxford Dominoes series. His other Oxford Bookworms titles at Stage 1 are *England* and *London* (Factfiles), *Goodbye, Mr Hollywood* (Thriller and Adventure), and *Sister Love and Other Crime Stories* (Crime and Mystery).

OXFORD BOOKWORMS LIBRARY

Classics • Crime & Mystery • Factfiles • Fantasy & Horror
Human Interest • Playscripts • Thriller & Adventure
True Stories • World Stories

The OXFORD BOOKWORMS LIBRARY provides enjoyable reading in English, with a wide range of classic and modern fiction, non-fiction, and plays. It includes original and adapted texts in seven carefully graded language stages, which take learners from beginner to advanced level. An overview is given on the next pages.

All Stage 1 titles are available as audio recordings, as well as over eighty other titles from Starter to Stage 6. All Starters and many titles at Stages 1 to 4 are specially recommended for younger learners. Every Bookworm is illustrated, and Starters and Factfiles have full-colour illustrations.

The OXFORD BOOKWORMS LIBRARY also offers extensive support. Each book contains an introduction to the story, notes about the author, a glossary, and activities. Additional resources include tests and worksheets, and answers for these and for the activities in the books. There is advice on running a class library, using audio recordings, and the many ways of using Oxford Bookworms in reading programmes. Resource materials are available on the website <www.oup.com/elt/gradedreaders>.

The *Oxford Bookworms Collection* is a series for advanced learners. It consists of volumes of short stories by well-known authors, both classic and modern. Texts are not abridged or adapted in any way, but carefully selected to be accessible to the advanced student.

You can find details and a full list of titles in the *Oxford Bookworms Library Catalogue* and *Oxford English Language Teaching Catalogues*, and on the website <www.oup.com/elt/gradedreaders>.

THE OXFORD BOOKWORMS LIBRARY
GRADING AND SAMPLE EXTRACTS

STARTER • 250 HEADWORDS

present simple – present continuous – imperative –
can/cannot, must – *going to* (future) – simple gerunds ...

Her phone is ringing – but where is it?

Sally gets out of bed and looks in her bag. No phone. She looks under the bed. No phone. Then she looks behind the door. There is her phone. Sally picks up her phone and answers it. *Sally's Phone*

STAGE 1 • 400 HEADWORDS

... past simple – coordination with *and*, *but*, *or* –
subordination with *before*, *after*, *when*, *because*, *so* ...

I knew him in Persia. He was a famous builder and I worked with him there. For a time I was his friend, but not for long. When he came to Paris, I came after him – I wanted to watch him. He was a very clever, very dangerous man. *The Phantom of the Opera*

STAGE 2 • 700 HEADWORDS

... present perfect – *will* (future) – *(don't) have to*, *must not*, *could* –
comparison of adjectives – simple *if* clauses – past continuous –
tag questions – *ask/tell* + infinitive ...

While I was writing these words in my diary, I decided what to do. I must try to escape. I shall try to get down the wall outside. The window is high above the ground, but I have to try. I shall take some of the gold with me – if I escape, perhaps it will be helpful later. *Dracula*

STAGE 3 • 1000 HEADWORDS

... should, may – present perfect continuous – *used to* – past perfect
– causative – relative clauses – indirect statements ...

Of course, it was most important that no one should see
Colin, Mary, or Dickon entering the secret garden. So Colin
gave orders to the gardeners that they must all keep away
from that part of the garden in future. *The Secret Garden*

STAGE 4 • 1400 HEADWORDS

*... past perfect continuous – passive (simple forms) –
would* conditional clauses – indirect questions –
relatives with *where/when* – gerunds after prepositions/phrases ...

I was glad. Now Hyde could not show his face to the world
again. If he did, every honest man in London would be proud
to report him to the police. *Dr Jekyll and Mr Hyde*

STAGE 5 • 1800 HEADWORDS

... future continuous – future perfect –
passive (modals, continuous forms) –
would have conditional clauses – modals + perfect infinitive ...

If he had spoken Estella's name, I would have hit him. I was so
angry with him, and so depressed about my future, that I could
not eat the breakfast. Instead I went straight to the old house.
Great Expectations

STAGE 6 • 2500 HEADWORDS

... passive (infinitives, gerunds) – advanced modal meanings –
clauses of concession, condition

When I stepped up to the piano, I was confident. It was as if I
knew that the prodigy side of me really did exist. And when I
started to play, I was so caught up in how lovely I looked that
I didn't worry how I would sound. *The Joy Luck Club*

BOOKWORMS · FACTFILES · STAGE 1
London
JOHN ESCOTT

Come with us to London – a city as old as the Romans, and as new as the twenty-first century. There are places to go – from Oxford Street to Westminster Abbey, from Shakespeare's Globe Theatre to Wimbledon Tennis Club. And things to do – ride on the London Eye, visit the markets, go to the theatre, run in the London Marathon. Big, beautiful, noisy, exciting – that's London.

BOOKWORMS · FACTFILES · STAGE 1
England
JOHN ESCOTT

Twenty-five million people come to England every year, and some never go out of London. But England too is full of interesting places to visit and things to do. There are big noisy cities with great shops and theatres, and quiet little villages. You can visit old castles and beautiful churches – or go to festivals with music twenty-four hours a day. You can have an English afternoon tea, walk on long white beaches, watch a great game of football, or visit a country house. Yes, England has something for everybody – what has it got for you?